Organ Transplantation

Andrew Campbell

FRANKLIN WATTS
LONDON • SYDNEY

First published in 2008 by Franklin Watts

Franklin Watts
338 Euston Road
London NW1 3BH

Franklin Watts Australia
Level 17/207 Kent Street
Sydney NSW 2000

A CIP catalogue record for this book
is available from the British Library.

Dewey number: 617.9'5

ISBN: 978 0 7496 8271 2

Printed in China

Franklin Watts is a division of Hachette Children's Books,
an Hachette Livre UK company.
www.hachettelivre.co.uk

Editor: Sarah Ridley
Design: Billin Design Solutions
Editor in Chief: John C. Miles
Art Director: Jonathan Hair
Picture research: Diana Morris

Picture credits:
Action Press/Rex Features: 21. Bettmann/Corbis: 11b, 12t. CHU Amiens/epa/Corbis: 39. Fabrice Coffrini/AFP/Getty Images: 2-3, 34. Custom Medical Stock/Science Photo Library: 1, 14, 48. Mike Devlin/Science Photo Library: 20. Owen Franklin/Corbis: 35. Patrick Frilet/Rex Features: 30. Garo/Phanie/Rex Features: 25. Hulton-Deutsch/Corbis: 29. Vincent Jannink/AFP/Getty Images: 15. Helen King/Corbis: cover. MBC/Keystone USA/Rex Features: 13b. Daniele La Monaca/Reuters/Corbis: 9. Hank Morgan/Science Photo Library: 26. Newspix: 19. Nottingham University Hospitals: 36. Scott Olsen/Getty Images: 17. Alfredo dagli Orti/San Marco Florence/The Art Archive: 10t. José Luis Pelaez/Blend Images/Getty Images: 18. Mark Peterson/Corbis: 28, 46-47. Philippe Plailly/Eurelios/Science Photo Library: 27. Chris Priest/Science Photo Library: 16. Rex Features: 24, 32. Gary Roberts/Rex Features: 22. Science Faction/Getty Images: 8. Sipa Press/Rex Features: 33, 38tl, 38tr. Transplant Sweden: 37. Voisin/Phanie/Rex Features: 23. Wales News Service: 31. Warner Brothers/Kobal/The Picture Desk: 40.

CONTENTS

INTRODUCTION

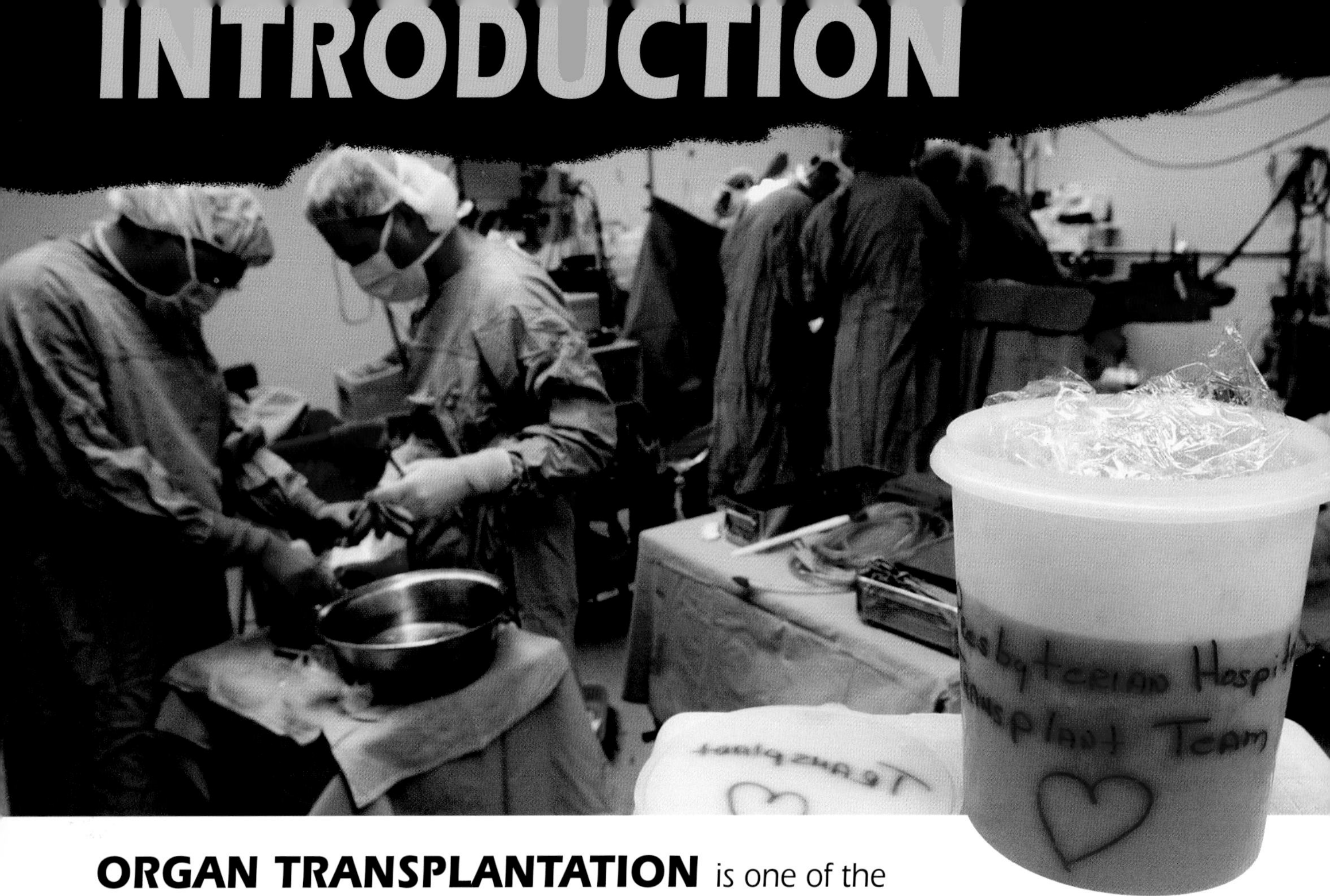

▲ A hospital heart transplant team at work in an operating theatre.

ORGAN TRANSPLANTATION is one of the biggest success stories of modern medicine. People of all ages have had their lives dramatically improved by receiving new organs to replace diseased or damaged ones. It is also one of the most controversial topics in medicine, both because of boundary-stretching procedures and discoveries and, more pressingly, a worldwide shortage of donated organs.

BREAKTHROUGHS

There have been many advances in organ transplantation since the first successful kidney transplant in 1954. Today, many donated kidneys continue to function well over ten years after surgery, while three-quarters of heart transplant patients survive for more than five years after their operation. New developments are rarely far from the headlines. In 2005, for example, French surgeons carried out the world's first partial face transplant.

VICTIM OF ITS OWN SUCCESS?

As medical research and surgical procedures improve, so more of us are able to benefit from organ transplants. The trouble is that the supply of donated organs cannot keep up with the demand for them. According to the World Health Organization, in 2005 approximately 66,000 people received kidney transplants – but ten times that number of people remained on kidney transplant waiting lists.

HOT TOPIC

There are many different responses to the issue of organ shortage, but each one has its own problems. While scientists develop artificial organs and explore the possibility of growing new ones from stem cells, health officials consider how to ensure that more people donate organs after death. Some individuals take matters into their own hands and buy organs illegally, often from poor and desperate people in developing countries.

GET THE FACTS STRAIGHT

An organ transplant involves the removal of body cells, tissue or a complete organ from its original site in the body and its transfer to a new position in the same person, or someone else. Transplants take place for a number of reasons:

- If an organ is irreversibly damaged by disease and cannot be treated by medicine or surgery;
- If an organ is so damaged because of an accident that it cannot be repaired;
- If an organ in a baby has failed to develop properly and surgery cannot repair it.

► New Zealand All Black rugby union star Jonah Lomu, who had a kidney transplant in 2004.

IN THE BEGINNING

THE IDEA of transplanting organs is ancient. The Bible tells how God created Eve from one of Adam's ribs, and stories about transplants survive from ancient Greece, Rome and China. The practice of skin transplants dates back more than 2,000 years, but it took a series of scientific discoveries in the 20th century to make the successful transplanting of internal organs a reality.

▲ This early 16th-century wood panel painting shows saints Cosmas and Damian performing a miraculous leg transplant.

THE EARLIEST NOSE JOB

The earliest plausible description of a transplant comes from the Indian surgeon Sushruta, who lived in the 2nd century BCE. He described a procedure for using skin grafts from a person's cheek to reconstruct the nose. These skin transplants are an example of autografts, where tissue is taken from one part of the body and used elsewhere. The first known homograft – transplanting tissue from one body to a different one – did not happen until 1905, when Dr Eduard Zirm of Moravia (Czech Republic) transplanted the part of the eye called the cornea.

GET THE FACTS STRAIGHT

Accounts of organ and body part transplants exist in ancient Chinese and early Christian writings, among other sources. Whether these accounts are anything more than colourful stories is anyone's guess.

In China in the 5th century BCE, the surgeon Pien Ch-iao reputedly exchanged the hearts of two men. One had a strong spirit but weak will, the other a strong will but weak spirit. Pien Ch-iao performed the operation to create balance in each man.

In Rome in the 3rd or 4th century CE, reports tell of the saints Damian and Cosmas replacing the wounded leg of a church official called Justinian with the leg of a man who had just died.

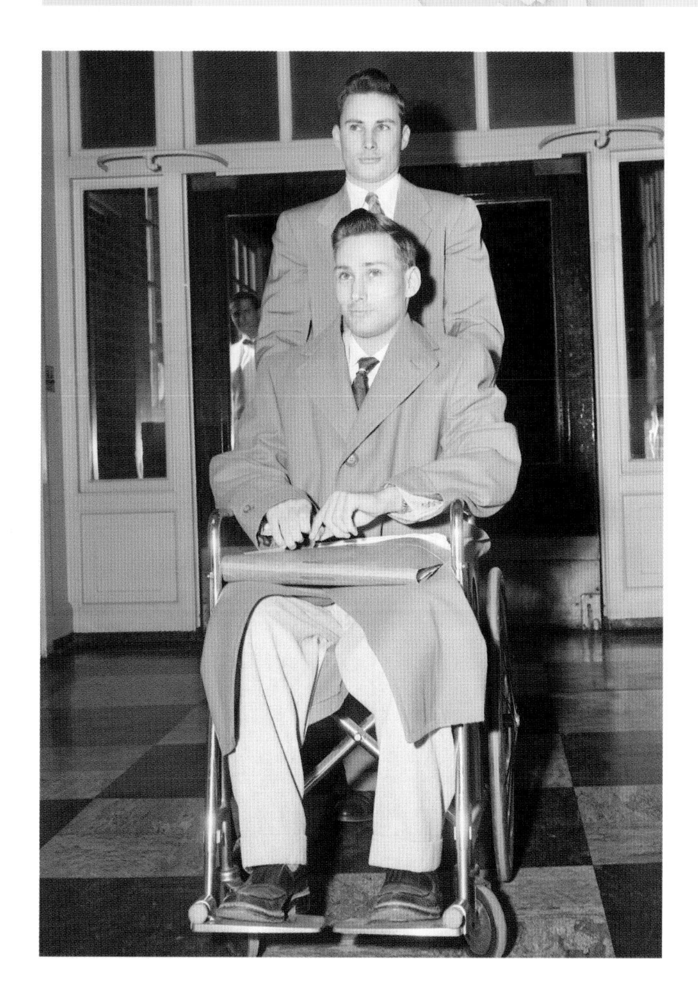

▲ Identical twins Richard and Ronald Herrick, the first participants in a successful kidney transplant in Boston, USA, in 1954.

REJECTION

Skin grafts and cornea transplants worked because they avoided the two biggest obstacles to the progress of organ transplantation. The first was joining a patient's blood vessels to his or her new organ. The French surgeon Alexis Carrel overcame this in the early 1900s. The second obstacle is the process known as rejection, when the body's immune system recognises tissue as foreign and attacks it. Understanding how our immune systems work was one of the major breakthroughs of 20th-century medicine.

THE HERRICK TWINS

Attempts were made to transplant major organs in the 1930s and 1940s, but rejection occurred each time. Then, in 1954 in Boston, USA, Dr Joseph Murray successfully transplanted a kidney from 23-year-old Ronald Herrick into his identical twin, Richard. Because both twins were genetically the same, Richard's body did not reject his brother's organ, and he lived for another eight years.

WORLD FIRSTS

THE STORY of organ transplants since the 1950s is one of incredible achievements and disappointing setbacks, many of which have captured the attention of newspaper and TV audiences around the world. Breakthroughs keep happening all the time, as surgeons and scientists continue to push the boundaries of the possible – and perhaps the acceptable.

▲ Dr Christiaan Barnard (left) discusses the world's first successful heart transplant with two colleagues prior to appearing on US television on 24 December 1967.

LIVERS AND HEARTS

Building on Dr Joseph Murray's 1954 kidney transplant success, Dr Thomas Starzl performed the world's first liver transplant in Colorado, USA, in 1963. The invention of a heart-lung machine, to pump blood mechanically around the body while a heart is removed and another replaces it, paved the way for the first heart transplant. In 1967 Dr Christiaan Barnard performed the surgery on 55-year-old Louis Washkansky in Cape Town, South Africa. Washkansky survived for only 18 days, but Barnard's achievement was a milestone.

UPS AND DOWNS

The number of transplants – and the media's interest in them – declined in the 1970s because survival times for patients continued to be short. Then, in the early 1980s, came the introduction of Cyclosporin, an immunosuppressant drug that helped prevent organ rejection without fatally weakening the body's immune system. Survival rates improved, and surgeons began to perform successful multiple organ transplants and transplant a greater range of organs.

GET THE FACTS STRAIGHT

This table lists the first successful transplant operations for each human organ.

1905	Cornea	Olmutz, Moravia (Czech Republic)
1954	Kidney	Boston, USA
1956	Bone marrow	New York, USA
1963	Liver	Denver, USA
1967	Heart	Cape Town, South Africa
1981	Combined heart and lung	Stanford, USA
1986	Double lung	Toronto, Canada
1998	Larynx	Cleveland, USA
1998	Hand	Lyon, France
2003	Tongue	Vienna, Austria
2005	Partial face	Amiens, France

MULTIPLE ORGAN TRANSPLANTS

The first multiple organ transplant was a combined heart and lung procedure, in California, USA, in 1981. By 2004 surgical knowledge and new technology meant that surgeons were able to carry out a record-breaking eight-organ transplant on a baby girl from Genoa, Italy. Six-month-old Alessia di Matteo received a liver, two kidneys, a stomach, pancreas, large and small intestines and a spleen from a baby boy who had died of a heart condition. Doctors at Jackson Memorial Hospital in Miami, USA, carefully monitored Alessia after the operation, but she remained ill and died almost a year later.

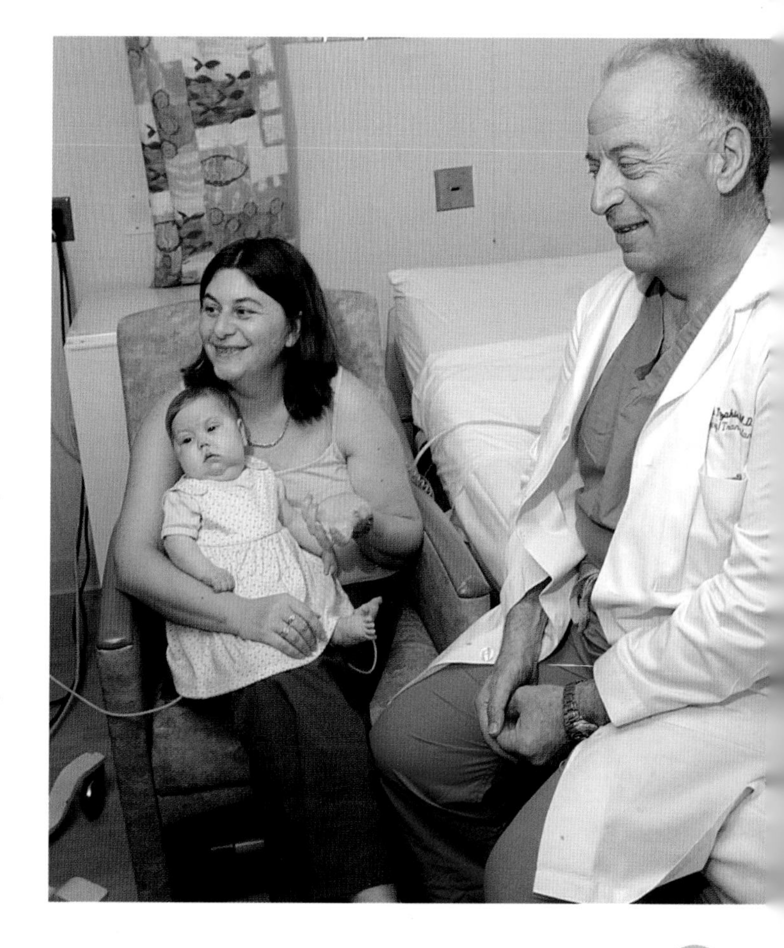

► Baby Alessia di Matteo, who received a record eight-organ transplant in 2004.

ORGAN CRISIS

THERE ARE THREE main sources of organs for transplantation: people who have died, living donors and other sources, including artificial organs and newly grown ones. The problem is that none of these sources is currently providing anything like enough organs for people who desperately need them. And those waiting for organs can die: in the USA around 16 people a day on organ waiting lists die before receiving a transplant.

GOOD NEWS AND BAD NEWS

As transplant surgery becomes increasingly effective, people live for longer and the incidence of kidney failure goes up, so the need for donated organs rises. Yet in Western countries at least, death rates among young people – whose organs are the most suitable for transplants – have fallen. Reasons for this drop include improvements in road safety and advances in preventing strokes among younger people.

PROFESSIONAL BUSINESS

Health systems around the world do their utmost to use every precious organ as effectively as possible. Organ exchange programmes hold information about patients, and specialist transplant co-ordinators act as quickly as possible to match patients to donor organs when they become available. This can involve finding a match in the local area, elsewhere in the country or even internationally.

► A human organ is rushed to hospital ready for transplantation. Speed can save a life!

THE WAITING GAME

The growing gap between organs needed and organs available has led to longer waiting times for people who require transplants. Unfortunately, the longer people wait the worse their chances of post-transplant survival become, since they will be weaker by the time of the operation. Life can be very hard for people waiting for a new organ. People with kidney failure have to spend hours each week connected to a dialysis machine. Those with heart or lung conditions may have to lead very restricted lives as they do not have the strength to be more active.

▲ Shocking TV viewers into awareness – the cast of "The Big Donor Show" (see below).

FACING THE ISSUES

In June 2007 viewers were stunned when "De Grote Donorshow" (The Big Donor Show) aired on Dutch TV. The show promised viewers that a dying woman known as Lisa would decide which of three people, each of whom had kidney disease, would receive her kidney after her death.

The production company behind the show was owned by Endemol, the makers of the TV show "Big Brother", which added to fears that an extremely sensitive subject was being reduced to a tacky reality-TV spectacle. But at the end of the programme the presenter, Patrick Lodiers, revealed the whole thing was a hoax, designed to publicise the shortage of kidney donors in the Netherlands.

As Lodiers himself said, it was "reality that was shocking" because about 200 people a year in the Netherlands die whilst waiting for a kidney transplant operation.

PRESUMED CONSENT

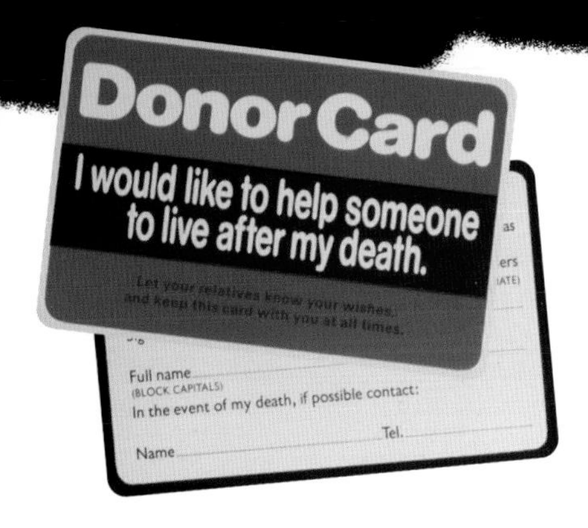

▲ The United Kingdom operates a Donor Card scheme. Organ donors carry the above card in their wallet or purse.

THE BIGGEST SOURCE of transplant organs comes from people who have died. The organs from a healthy person who has died in an accident, for example, may benefit several different people. But for that to happen the victim would have had to be on a donor register, and the relatives would have to agree to the surgeons' request to use his or her organs. Alternatively, the victim would have to live in a country that presumes organs can be used for transplants unless a person has specifically refused this.

DONOR REGISTRATION

Countries such as the USA, Australia and the UK operate donor registration schemes, which record information about people who have decided to donate their organs when they die. In the UK about 13 million people – or one in five of the population – are on the National Health Service's Organ Donor Register. In Australia about 5 million people – or one in four of the population – have registered their intention or consent to donate organs.

FAMILY CHOICES

Despite the large numbers of people on donor registration schemes, the organ shortage continues. One problem is that a dead person's relatives can often refuse their consent to the removal of their loved one's organs. This refusal may come because the dead person never informed family members of his or her wishes when alive. Relatives might also refuse permission on religious grounds or because they are simply too traumatised to think about a surgeon cutting up their loved one's body.

THE OTHER WAY ROUND

An alternative to donor registration is presumed consent, which effectively turns the system on its head. In this system, everyone is considered a willing donor unless they specifically register a refusal while alive. Countries such as Norway, Spain, Israel and France have laws based on presumed consent, and advocates say its success speaks for itself: Spain has 35 organ donors for every million people, three times the UK rate of 12.9 per million. Opponents argue that some people may not understand that they can opt out of consenting.

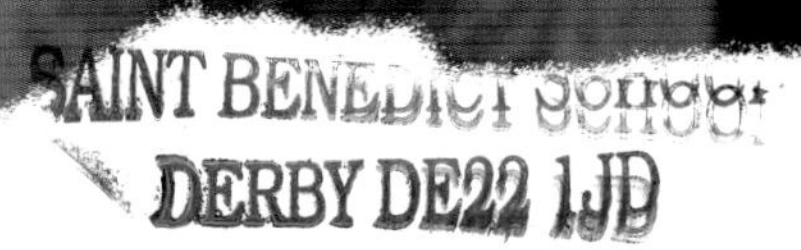

FACING THE ISSUES

One of the most important people involved in any transplant is the transplant co-ordinator, who acts as the link between the patient and the family of the deceased. The importance of this role is proven in Spain. In the early 1990s about 30% of families refused permission - despite presumed consent - for the organs of their relatives to be used in transplants.

By 2007, thanks largely to a network of transplant co-ordinators working in hospitals, this refusal rate had halved to about 15%. Co-ordinators, such as Professor Jose Ramon Nunez who works in Madrid's San Carlos Hospital, ask families to think what their loved one would have wanted to happen to his or her body. "We need to be very clear with them about the importance of the decision they're going to make," Nunez says. "Another life may depend on them saying yes or no."

▼ Mourners at a funeral. Unfortunately the best source of organs suitable for transplantation is from young people who have died.

LIFE FROM LIFE

ORGAN SHORTAGES around the world have led to an increase in living donors, people who donate an organ, or part of an organ, that they can live healthily without. This includes a kidney, a lung or part of the liver, as well as blood or bone marrow. Around one in four of all kidney transplants now comes from living donors.

BENEFITS

Organs from living donors have some distinct advantages over those from the deceased. The patient receiving the organ will usually get it sooner from a living donor than if they had to wait for the right match from someone who had died. This means their bodies are less likely to get weaker, and their chances of recovery are better. Another plus is that living donation can occur at the same hospital as the recipient, ruling out delays, and at a time that best suits the well-being of both donor and recipient.

RISKS

All surgery carries a risk, and hospital transplant teams need to be sure that potential donors understand what can go wrong. While studies show that kidney donors are no more likely than anyone else to develop kidney failure, if they do they will need a kidney transplant themselves. Another risk that transplant teams have to be very aware of is family pressure on a person to donate his or her organs. This pressure could lead to feelings of guilt or resentment later on, and if it is detected beforehand the transplant may well not take place.

► Medical staff need to explain very carefully to potential donors the risks involved in transplant operations.

WHO DONATES?

Most living donors tend to be close family members, since they often have the strongest motivation and their organ or tissue is likely to be the best match. However, husbands, wives, partners and friends also donate their organs. Other living donors can be transplant patients. In the world's first "domino transplant" in the USA in 1987, Clinton House received a new heart and lungs from a road accident victim. House's own healthy heart was transplanted into another man.

► David McKay (left), the founder of the Jesus Christians, and group member Ashwyn Falkingham. In 2007 a hospital in Toronto, Canada, refused to accept Falkingham's offer to donate one of his kidneys – his mother had told the hospital she thought he had been brainwashed by the cult.

WHAT DO YOU THINK?

Most living donors donate an organ to someone they know. An Australian religious group called the Jesus Christians, however, encourages members to donate organs to strangers. The tiny group practises what it preaches: in 2006, 15 of its 28 members donated one of their kidneys. The state government of Victoria in Australia has banned the Jesus Christians from donating any more organs after reports that the group's leader, David McKay, had forced followers to donate. Other countries, particularly in Europe, also ban religious groups from donating organs in this way.

THE ACT of taking part of one person's body and putting it into someone else's arouses concerns over what is right and wrong. Often it is the doctors and scientists who must decide for themselves in the first instance, leaving the rest of us to debate the situation afterwards.

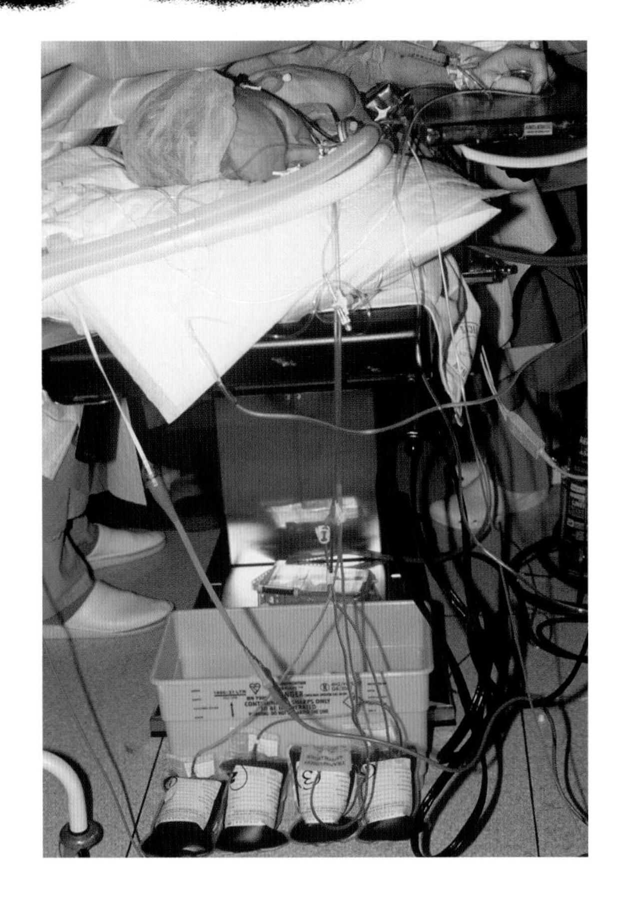

▲ Surgeons performing "bloodless surgery" on a Jehovah's Witness.

RELIGIOUS HARMONY

Most of the world's religions have little problem with the idea of organ donation and transplantation, as long as it is carried out appropriately and respectfully. Many Christians, for instance, regard organ donation as an act of compassion, while many Muslims see it as part of the Koranic instruction to save life. Even Jehovah's Witnesses, whose religious laws rule against accepting blood transfusions, endorse organ transplants if surgery is performed without the use of transfusions. Surgeons have now developed a special bloodless procedure for Jehovah's Witness transplant patients.

BRAIN-STEM DEATH

There is more uncertainty over removing organs from people who are not technically dead. Such people include coma victims who are in a persistent vegetative state, and who are only kept alive by machines that control their blood flow and breathing. Doctors must obey very strict guidelines to determine if these patients are "brain dead" before preparing to use their organs for transplantation. Even so, many religious groups are divided over the medical definition of death, and some even describe the removal of organs from patients in such a condition as an act of murder.

TRADITIONAL VIEWS

Culture and community, as well as religion, can also influence people's attitudes to organ donation and transplantation. Among African-Caribbean and Asian communities in the UK, refusal rates for donating a relative's organs are twice as high as among white communities. Religious and traditional reasons are often given as the reason, despite the fact that African-Caribbean and south-east Asian peoples are three times more likely to have kidney failure and to need an organ transplant themselves.

▲ Pope Benedict XVI, a cautious advocate for organ transplantation (see panel below).

GET THE FACTS STRAIGHT

The American Red Cross presents the views of all mainstream faith groups towards organ transplantation on its website. Here are the views of three religions:

Roman Catholic

Catholics view organ donation as an act of charity, fraternal love and self-sacrifice. Pope John Paul II (the pope before Benedict XVI) said: "Those who believe in our Lord Jesus Christ, who gave His life for the salvation of all, should recognise the urgent need for a ready availability of organs for transplants [as] a challenge to their generosity and fraternal love."

Islam

The Muslim Religious Council initially rejected organ donation by followers of Islam in 1983 but has reversed its position, provided that donors consent in writing in advance. The organs of Muslim donors must be transplanted immediately and not be stored in organ banks.

Judaism

Judaism teaches that saving a human life takes precedence over maintaining the sanctity of the human body. According to New York rabbi Moses Tendler: "If one is in the position to donate an organ to save another's life, it is obligatory to do so, even if the donor never knows who the beneficiary will be."

Source: http://www.redcross.org/donate/tissue/relgstmt.html

ARTIFICIAL ORGANS

◀ The Jarvik 2000 artificial heart was much smaller and lighter than earlier models.

THE WORLD'S first artificial heart, in 1982, brought with it the hope that artificial organs could be the answer to the two biggest problems in organ transplantation: organ shortage and rejection. But the recipient of that first mechanical heart lived only another 112 days, and subsequent man-made organs have failed to work well enough or simply been too bulky to use. Scientists admit they still have a long way to go with this research.

HEART OF THE MATTER

Milestones in the development of an effective artificial heart include the Jarvik 2000 – named after the 1982 model, the Jarvik-7, made by Robert Jarvik of Utah, USA. The much smaller Jarvik 2000 used a turbine to boost the power of each heartbeat. The first patient to receive one, Peter Houghton from Birmingham, UK, survived another five months. The so-called Berlin Heart, first developed in 1990, sits outside the body and helps either ventricle, or pumping chamber, to pump blood. Unlike other artificial heart devices, it can be made as small as a golf ball and so can help babies with heart defects.

PUMPING AND PUFFING

Scientists are also working to develop artificial livers, lungs and kidneys. Artificial livers contain a mechanical pump to push blood through the machine, as well as human liver cells to break down toxins in the blood and produce vital chemicals. Artificial lung devices include intravenous membrane oxygenators, or IMOs, which contain a balloon that inflates and deflates to circulate oxygen and remove carbon dioxide. Artificial kidney research lags behind work on these two organs.

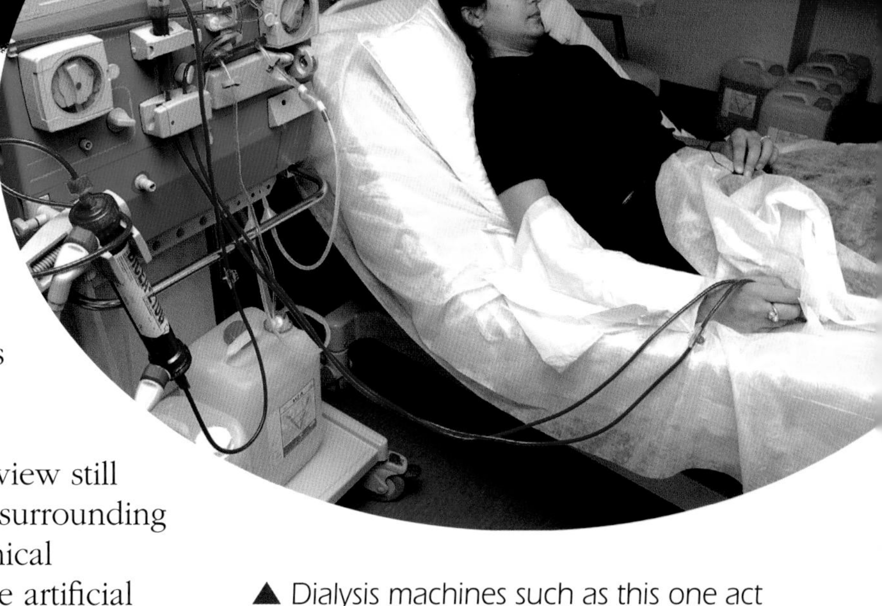

OPEN FIELD

Artificial organ research is a constantly evolving field. Because of the limited long-term success of early devices, scientists and surgeons began to see artificial organs as only temporary measures while a patient waited for a human transplant. This view still holds, but there is much excitement surrounding hybrid organs which contain mechanical elements with living cells, such as the artificial liver. It may be that these hybrid devices hold the key to solving the organ shortage crisis.

▲ *Dialysis machines such as this one act as substitute kidneys for adults and young people with kidney disease.*

FACING THE ISSUES

Dialysis machines may not spring to mind when you think of artificial organs, but for patients with kidney failure they act as substitute kidneys.They can also rule patients' lives. Charlene Henry, from Newcastle, UK, describes life on dialysis:

> "I became diagnosed with kidney failure just after my 16th birthday. I was in hospital for two weeks and I lost a lot of weight because I couldn't eat anything that I liked and most of my weight was fluid to start with. Before I was diagnosed I was seven stone and when I dialysed I went right down to four-and-a-half stone. Being on dialysis is sometimes very frustrating because you have to watch what you eat and drink constantly. Having to do this is very hard for most people as they might only have 350 ml to drink a day and they might not be able to have treats like some other children. [The other children in my ward and I] all go to dialysis three times a week. I am normally on my machine for about three-and-a-half hours unless I have extra, and I have to be on my machine for as long as it takes to get the extra fluid off. Having to go onto dialysis three times a week is very tiring, as I have to go to sixth form, then on to dialysis. I only have four days off from dialysis and I think they are the best days of the week."

Source: http://www.kidney.org.uk/perceptions/charlene-henry.html

Reproduced with kind permission of the National Kidney Federation and Charlene Henry.

XENOTRANSPLANTATION

XENOTRANSPLANTATION is the use of animal organs, instead of human ones, for transplant. In the 1990s xenotransplantation was the buzzword of the scientific community, seen as the ultimate solution to the worldwide organ shortage. Today, these hopes have been all but dashed as the ethical concerns and health risks of this research have proved too great.

STORMS OF CONTROVERSY

In the 1980s xenotransplantation research identified pigs as the most suitable animal for transplanted organs. Their organs are similar in size to our own, and are fairly easy to genetically alter to be more human. The first problem the scientists ran into, however, was the ethical debate about whether it was right to modify pigs' genes in the first place. Then, before pig organ transplants into humans could go ahead, researchers transplanted the organs into primates such as baboons, monkeys and chimpanzees. Animal rights campaigners were appalled at the suffering this inflicted on the primates.

▼ *Animal rights activists campaign against scientific experiments involving primates.*

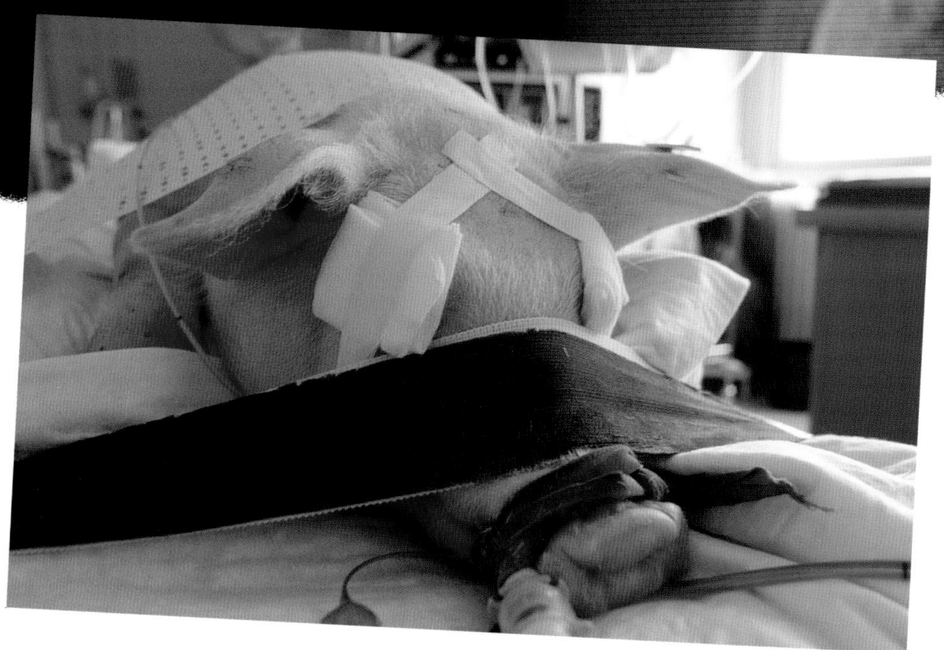

◄ A pig undergoes a laboratory test. Campaigners vehemently oppose xeno-transplantation on the grounds of the suffering caused to pigs, primates and other animals.

PIGS MIGHT FLY

The final nail in the coffin of xenotransplantation – at least for now – is the fear that the process might be extremely dangerous for human health. Researchers discovered that a pig virus called porcine endogenous retrovirus, which is harmless to pigs, has the ability to infect human cells. Knowledge of HIV, the virus that causes AIDS, shows that when certain viruses jump from one species to another they become deadly, as HIV did when it crossed from monkeys to humans. This is a risk that no-one wants to take with the pig virus.

FARMYARD PHARMACIES

The answer to the organ crisis might not come from whole-organ transplants from other animals. However, tissue from other animals is regularly used to save human lives. Since 1975 and 1981 respectively, pig and cow heart valves have been used to replace damaged human heart valves. In addition, surgeons use sheep intestines for surgical stitches, and cow tendons and bones to replace human ones damaged in accidents.

GET THE FACTS STRAIGHT

The idea of xenotransplantation, like that of organ transplantation in general, is not new:

- In 1667, English surgeon Dr Richard Lower gave a "melancholic" patient a transfusion of lamb's blood. The patient apparently survived.
- In 1906, French surgeon Mathieu Jaboulay transplanted a goat's liver into one woman and a pig's kidney into another. Both women died.
- In 1964, Dr James Hardy of Mississippi, USA, transplanted a chimpanzee's heart into a 68-year-old man. The patient died after 90 minutes.
- In 1984, surgeons in California, USA, transplanted a baboon's heart into a baby girl, Fae. She survived for three weeks.

STEM CELL RESEARCH

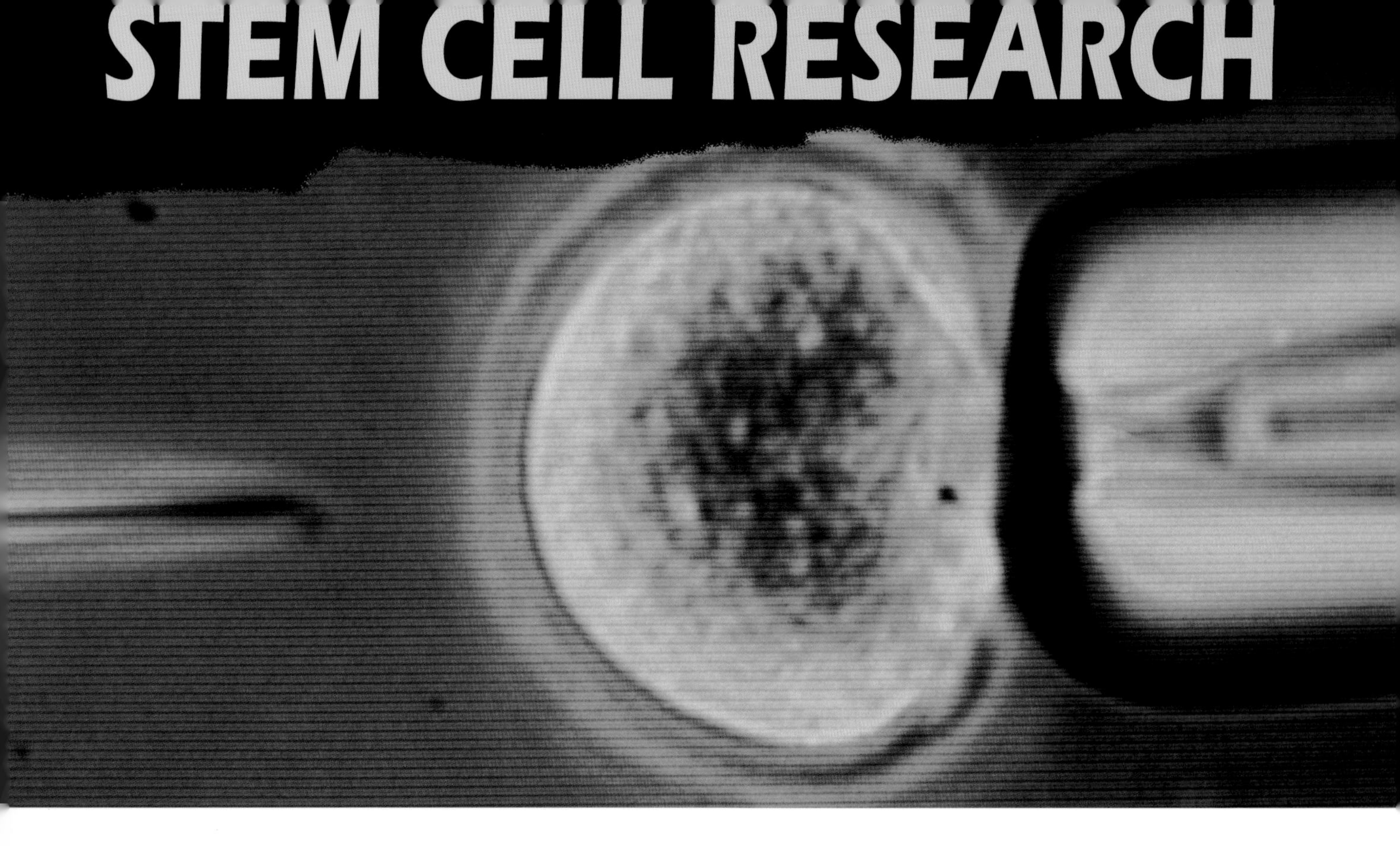

▲ This electronic image shows a cell (centre) about to be injected with DNA to alter it.

STEM CELLS are cells that have the potential to develop into each and every type of cell in the body. Much scientific research focuses on using stem cells to grow new body parts, including organs. This research could one day revolutionise not only organ transplantation but the whole of medicine – but it is not without practical or ethical problems.

OVERVIEW

The basic idea is that scientists take stem cells from a patient and stimulate those cells to grow into a new organ to replace a diseased or damaged one. Besides overcoming the need to wait for a donor organ, this would also deal with the problem of rejection as the new organ would come from the patient's own body and would not therefore be attacked as foreign matter.

STUMBLING BLOCKS

But one of the key difficulties in stem cell research is obtaining the stem cells in the first place. Stem cells in adults are fairly limited in the cell types they can develop into. Stem cells in newborn babies have much more potential. One solution would be to store stem cells from every baby, which could be used if the individual needed them at some time in his or her life.

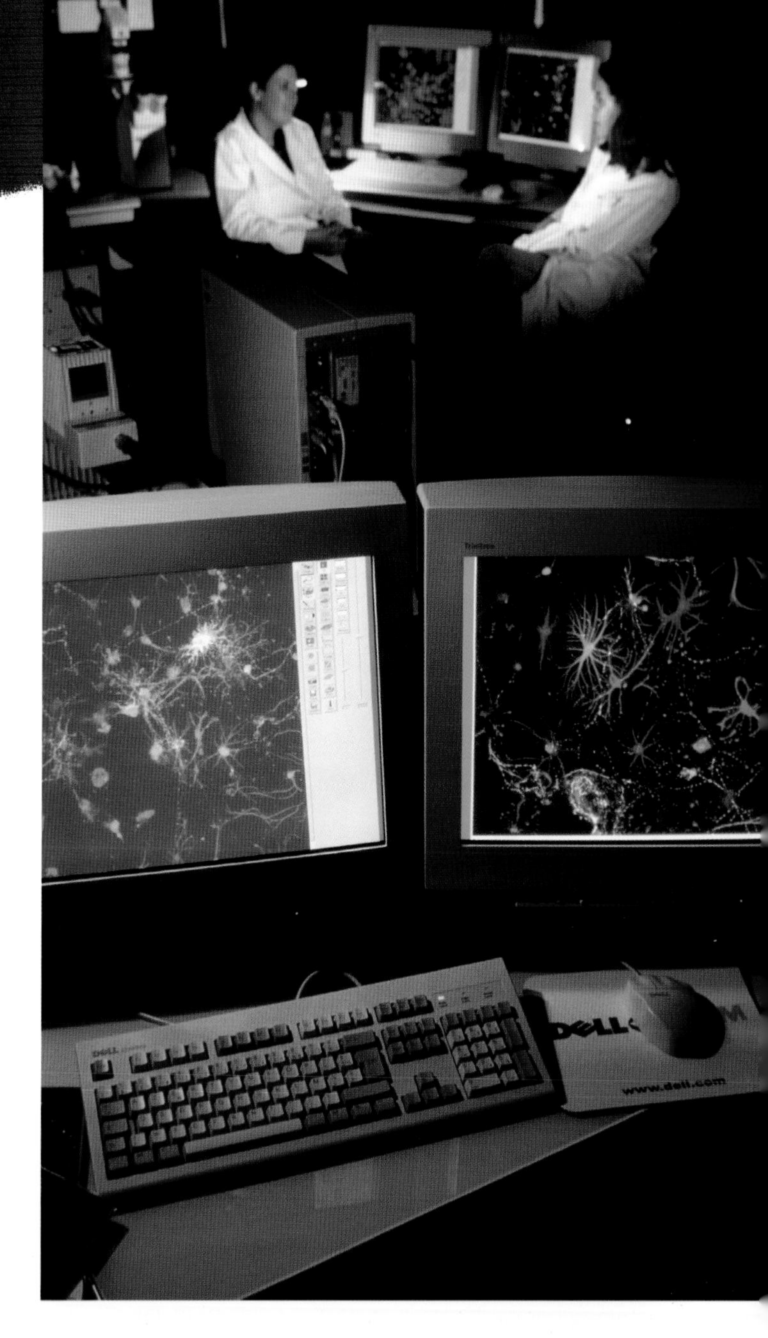

Another source of stem cells is from human embryos. After much debate, governments in countries such as the USA and the UK have decided to allow embryonic stem cell research, but many people are strongly opposed to using potential human beings in this way.

BRANCHING OUT

Other cell research could be of benefit to people needing new organs. In 2006, scientists in North Carolina, USA, reported that they had taken bladder cells from patients and had successfully divided and multiplied them to grow new bladders. They then transplanted the new bladders into the patients. As with the hope for stem cells and new organs, there is no risk of rejection with this kind of transplantation.

► *Stem-cell research in progress at the Genethon facility in Evry, France. The computer displays in the foreground show micrographs of the cell cultures.*

WHAT DO YOU THINK?

- Some people think it is wrong to use human embryos for stem cell research, because the embryo cannot give its permission and its rights are therefore violated. What do you think of this argument?
- Do you think it is right for scientists to modify the genetic information in plant, animal or human cells – to "play God" with nature?
- What limits would you place on scientific research? Do you, for instance, think all research is justified if it aims to save or improve human life?

THE RIGHT TO AN ORGAN?

WHEN THE NEED for transplant organs outstrips availability, how do doctors decide which patients receive them? Is it simply a matter of who has been waiting the longest, or who needs an organ the most urgently? A hugely controversial issue is whether some people deserve organs more, or less, than others. This debate commonly focuses on alcoholics who need liver transplants.

DANGEROUS DRINKING

Our livers perform a range of vital body functions, including breaking down toxins and old blood cells, storing fats and producing blood-clotting factors. Alcoholic liver disease, brought on by chronic drinking, can irreversibly damage the organ, replacing functioning liver tissue with scar tissue.

Liver transplant units routinely screen people with the disease to decide if they will return to their dangerous drinking habits after receiving a new liver. If the unit decides there is a risk of this happening, they may refuse to go ahead with the transplant.

WHAT DO YOU THINK?

- Do you think everyone has an equal right to a new organ?
- Given that the supply of organs is limited, what about the argument that some people deserve organs more - for example, people who benefit society in some way?
- Do you think George Best deserved his new liver (see below)?
- How would you decide if someone was sincere about trying to stop drinking after receiving a liver transplant?

▲ George Best at the height of his football career in the 1960s.

FOOTBALL AND POLITICS

High-profile examples of this issue make the headlines from time to time. In 2003 former Northern Ireland and Manchester United footballer George Best was reported as going on a binge drinking session just 12 months after a life-saving liver transplant. Some people said the transplant was wasted on him. Best died in 2005. In 2007 critics of South Africa's health minister Manto Tshabalala-Msimang accused her of abusing her position to obtain a liver transplant, despite her failure to stop drinking. The critics claimed that doctors would normally have refused to give someone a new liver under such circumstances.

◀ Excessive drinking can lead to chronic liver disease. But who should receive a transplant?

THE BIGGER PICTURE

Refusing to give someone a new organ on the grounds that they have contributed to their condition is extremely problematic: the same could be said of people with heart or lung disease, as with liver disease. The question for doctors to decide is whether the patient will go on to damage their new organ or not. The general principle guiding organ allocation is that everyone has an equal right. But statistics suggest some people's rights are more "equal" than others. Better connected and wealthier people may well stand a better chance of obtaining an organ.

TRANSPLANT TOURISTS

AN ALTERNATIVE to waiting for a donor organ is to buy one from someone willing to sell you one of theirs. This might seem a reasonable solution if you are desperate or wealthy enough, but one problem is that buying and selling organs is illegal in most countries.

▼ Shanty housing in Mexico City. For some poor people in the developing world, the sale of a kidney represents one way of raising a lot of money.

MUST-HAVES

There is quite a history to the buying and selling of body parts. In 18th-century England, for example, rich patients with rotten teeth paid for teeth to be wrenched out of the mouths of poor people and implanted into their own mouths. Today, those who do buy organs are often wealthy and wish to avoid waiting in a queue with everyone else. But many others are ordinary people, simply desperate to have a new organ and a new start in life.

KIDNEYS FOR SALE

The organ trade is outlawed in all Western nations, but countries such as Pakistan and the Philippines do not impose a ban. Since people can, in the right conditions, function with one kidney as well as with two, the kidney is the main organ involved. So-called "transplant tourists" from Europe, Australia, the USA, Japan and the Middle East travel to developing countries where they can purchase a kidney for as little as £2,000.

CYBER ORGANS

The Internet offers another route to buying an organ. In 2004 the offer of a human kidney on eBay attracted bids as high as $5.7 million. eBay pulled the item from auction and informed the police. An eBay spokesman told journalists, "from time to time we get a kidney or liver".

FACING THE ISSUES

In 2007, 44-year-old Mark Schofield, a former surfing champion from South Wales, travelled to the Philippines to buy a new kidney.

After four-and-a-half years on the waiting list for a donor organ, Mark decided that he had had enough. He and his wife Jayne, a nurse, found a surgeon in Manila who promised to find someone who would sell them a kidney. The cost was estimated at about £40,000.

When asked by the BBC to respond to people who might criticise what he was doing on moral grounds, Mark responded, "If the people that are standing on the moral ground said what else I can do, I would trade places with them. You stick to your moral argument, but I'm not prepared to sit down, lie down and play dead."

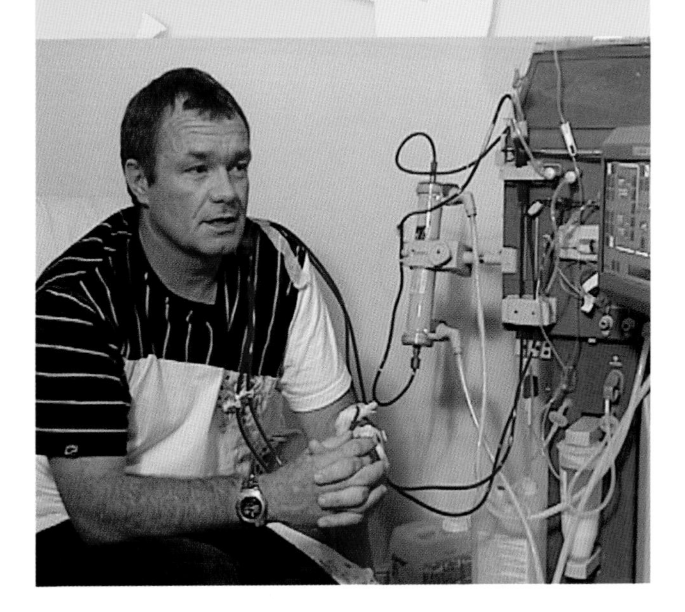

► Mark Schofield, who spent hours every day linked to a dialysis machine at his home in the UK.

ORGAN SELLERS

SOME PEOPLE argue that the organ trade is all about co-operation: one person gets a new organ while another makes some much-needed cash. But campaigners against the trade say that exploits the poor, and seriously threatens their health.

FORCED TO SELL

It is not just that most people who sell one of their organs are poor, it is that many feel forced into doing so because of debt. In parts of southern India that were devastated by the tsunami of 2004, journalists discovered women selling their kidneys to pay off loans they took out after their homes were destroyed. The pressure of these debts means that people like this have no real choice in selling their organs or not. It is the only way they can look after their families.

HEALTH COSTS

With the right diet and lifestyle, a person can live as well with one kidney as with two. But these conditions rarely apply in the developing countries where most organs are bought and sold. In 2002, the Journal of the American Medical Association published a study of 305 Indians who had sold their kidneys an average of six years earlier. The study found that 86% of these organ sellers reported declining health since their operation.

◀ Parts of southern India and Sri Lanka were devastated by the 2004 tsunami. People have sold kidneys to pay off rebuilding loans.

ORGANS TO ORDER?

One of the most sinister issues surrounding the sale of human organs concerns reports that transplant centres in China have sold the organs of executed prisoners. Accounts from journalists and doctors suggest that people from Japan, Korea and further afield have travelled to China to receive organ transplants from dead prisoners. In 2006 the Chinese government responded to international criticism by banning the buying and selling of organs. It has also claimed that organs have only ever been taken from prisoners with their consent.

▲ Members of China's banned Falun Gong religion have alleged that, in the past, adherents have been executed to provide organs for transplant.

FACING THE ISSUES

The international trade in illegal organs came under the spotlight in 2003, when police in Durban, South Africa, uncovered a criminal syndicate that spanned three continents. The brokers who organised the syndicate were based in Israel; they relied on poor donors from Brazil to sell their organs to those willing to pay. The illegal transplant operations then took place at the private transplant clinic of St Augustine's Hospital, Durban. One of the Brazilian "donors" alerted the South African police to the syndicate. The police set up a sting operation, which led to the arrests of the Israeli brokers and 12 Brazilians, as well as South African transplant surgeons and other medical personnel. Syndicates such as this may well be the tip of the iceberg and conceal the involvement of government officials around the world in allowing the illegal movement of donors, buyers and organs. It is likely that children have suffered as well as adults: there are claims that children from countries such as Mexico and Azerbaijan have been smuggled abroad as organ donors.

REGULATING THE TRADE

▲ The 2007 annual assembly meeting of the World Health Organization (WHO) in Geneva. The WHO is opposed to the illegal trade in organs.

ONE KEY question in the debate over the sale of organs is whether an outright ban – if it could ever be achieved – is the best approach, or whether, given the chronic shortage of organs, regulating the sale of body parts is actually in our best interests.

WHO'S DOING ANYTHING?

In 1991 the World Health Organization (WHO) issued guidelines to prevent the exploitation of people who sell their organs. A total of 192 countries signed up to these guidelines, but in practice a number of developing nations turn a blind eye to organ buying and selling. Many other countries back up the WHO guidelines with laws, such as the UK's Human Organ Transplant Act 1989. The success of these laws varies.

CAMPAIGNERS

The WHO actively seeks to end transplant tourism, arguing that the trade has the potential to exploit the poor and threaten people's health and lives. Since people may be forced into selling an organ through debt or another form of obligation, the WHO also believes that the trade can violate basic human rights. It is not alone in making this argument. Organs Watch was set up at the University of California, Berkeley, USA, in 1999 to monitor the illegal organ trade.

THE OTHER SIDE

Other people argue that the way to tackle the problem is not to ban the trade but to regulate it. US transplant specialists Eli Friedman and Amy Friedman suggest that kidneys should sell for a "fair price", which they put at around $40,000. Pricing organs like this would, they propose, bring an end to the black market, which rarely puts people's health first. The British kidney surgeon Dr Andy Stein agrees with this, claiming that the shortage of organs justifies legalising the trade.

WHAT DO YOU THINK?

- Do you think the buying and selling of organs can be justified?
- If the trade were to be regulated, what safeguards would you want to see put in place?
- Do you agree with the argument that selling a kidney can benefit someone who desperately needs the money?
- If you, or someone you cared about, needed a new kidney, would you accept having to go on a waiting list to receive it, even if waiting times could be several years?

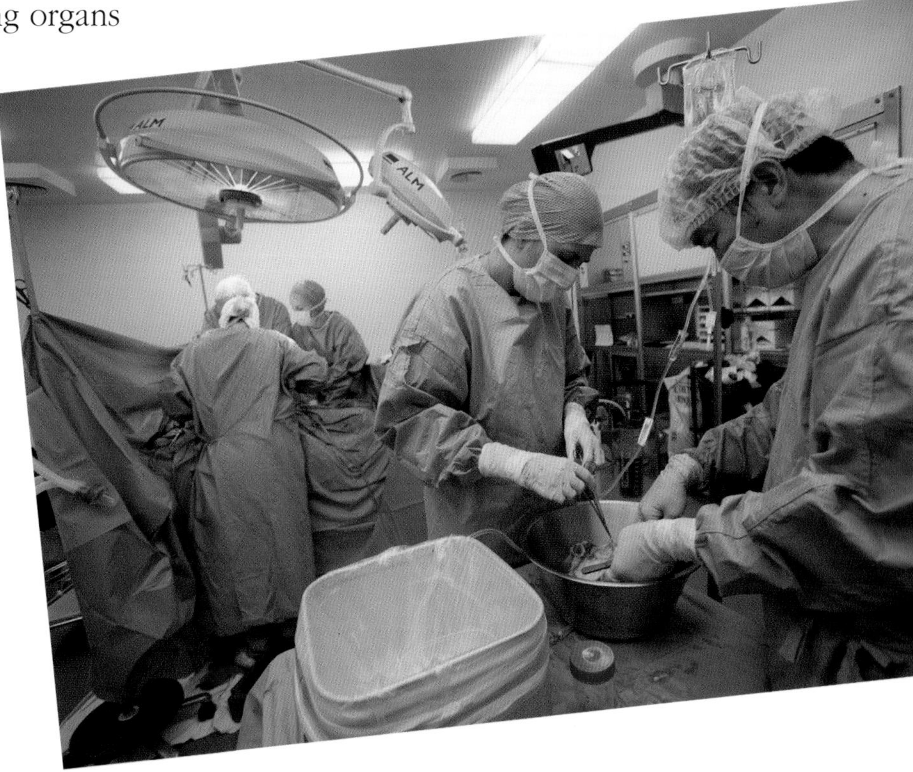

► A kidney transplant team operates. Some people argue that the trade in kidneys for transplant should be regulated.

POST-OPERATIVE LIFE

TODAY, the outlook for people who have undergone an organ transplant is generally good: surgical techniques, tissue matching and immunosuppressant drugs have all improved since the early days of transplantation. Living with part of someone else inside you, however, can create practical and emotional difficulties.

▲ Champion badminton player Peter Murray of Sheffield, UK, who underwent a kidney transplant in 1995.

PHYSICAL EFFECTS

Immediately after a transplant operation a patient will remain in hospital while doctors carry out a series of tests and checks to ensure the new organ is working properly and oversee the dosage of immunosuppressants to prevent rejection. The downside to these drugs is that the patient is vulnerable to infection and may need to take antibiotics to counter this. After leaving hospital, the patient will need to return for regular check-ups. Many patients will require check-ups at least once a year for the rest of their lives.

PSYCHOLOGICAL EFFECTS

Many people experience a wide range of emotions after receiving a donated organ. Feelings of relief and happiness are natural; so too can be depression at the years lost because of ill health. People can also have mixed feelings towards their new organs. In 2000, two years after his groundbreaking hand transplant, New Zealander Clint Hallam asked surgeons to remove it. Hallam said that the hand, which came from a dead motorcyclist, felt like a dead man's hand and he had no sense it now belonged to him.

LIVING DONORS

Most living donors feel very positive after their operation. When a person donates a kidney, for example, to a family member and can see the benefits of their act, these feelings are reinforced. If the transplant procedure does not work or there are complications, other emotions such as guilt or resentment may surface. On the physical side, studies show that organ donors actually live longer than the average population. This may be, however, because donors tend to be selected on the basis that they have a good level of health.

GET THE FACTS STRAIGHT

Every two years, the World Transplant Games attracts competitors from all over the world who have had a transplant. Founded in 1978, the Games celebrate the success of organ transplants and the full lives that recipients can live, and publicise the need for more organ donations. The Games have been held in New York, Athens, Amsterdam, Singapore, Budapest, Vancouver and Manchester, and have led individual countries, including the UK, Australia, France and the USA, to establish their own national transplant games as well. The honorary chairman of the 2004 US Transplant Games was Dr Joseph Murray, who performed the first successful kidney transplantation 50 years earlier (see page 11).

► The Swedish team pose for a photo at the World Transplant Games in Bangkok, 2007.

FACE TRANSPLANTS

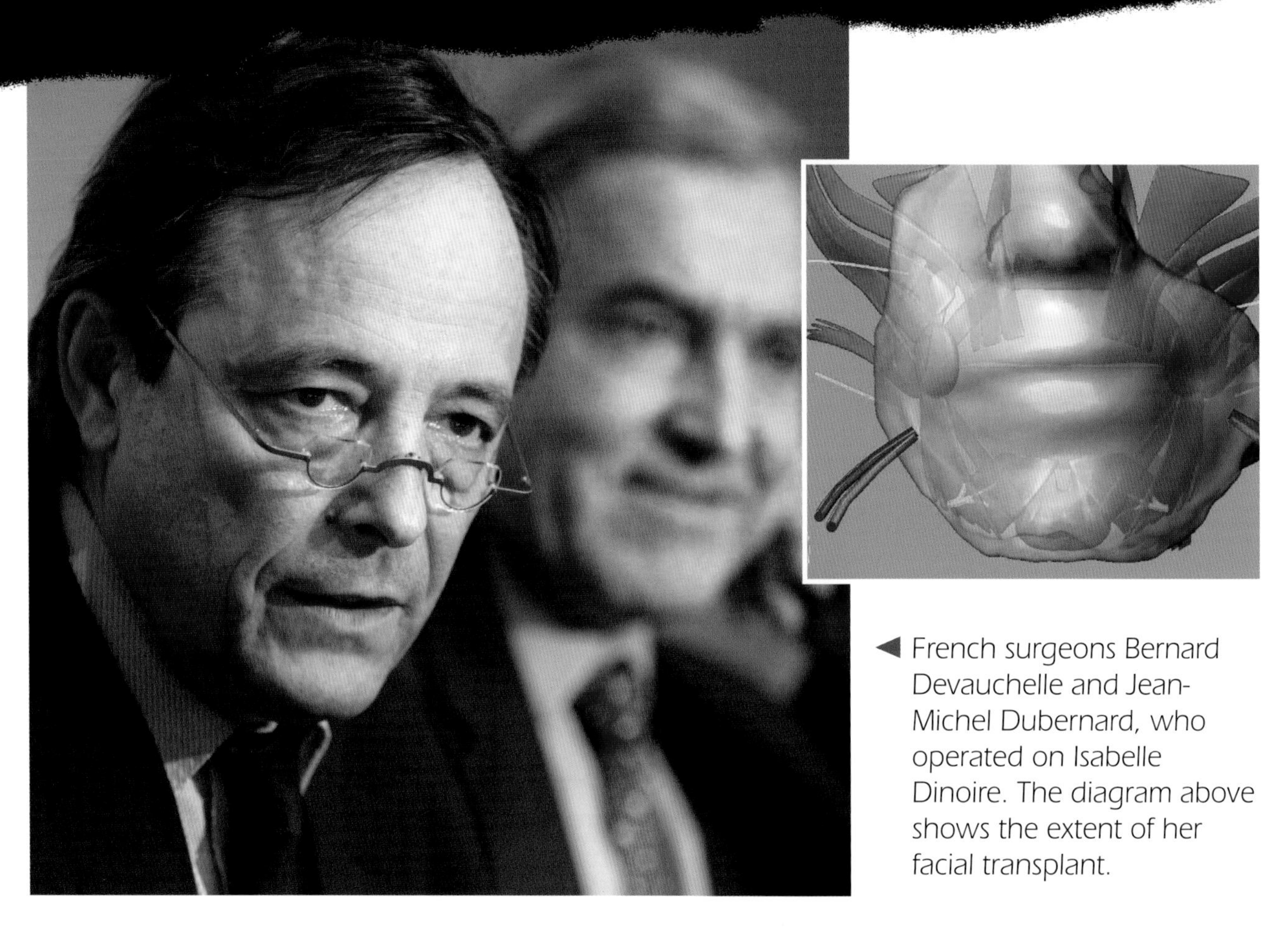

◄ French surgeons Bernard Devauchelle and Jean-Michel Dubernard, who operated on Isabelle Dinoire. The diagram above shows the extent of her facial transplant.

ON 27 NOVEMBER 2005 the boundaries of medical science and transplantation surgery were pushed one step further when a woman from Amiens in France underwent a partial face transplant. Isabelle Dinoire, then aged 38, had taken an overdose of sleeping pills. Unable to wake her up, Isabelle's pet dog had gone berserk and mauled her face, destroying her nose, chin and mouth.

UNKNOWN TERRITORY

Isabelle's surgeons decided that the untried procedure of a partial face transplant was the only option left to them. In an operation lasting 15 hours they transplanted the nose, chin and mouth from another woman who had committed suicide. The operation was a success, although the surgeons had to increase Isabelle's dose of immuno-suppressants to prevent her body from rejecting the new facial tissue. The high dosage Isabelle is on brings with it an increased risk of her developing cancer.

QUESTIONS, QUESTIONS

Some people criticised the surgeons for not attempting facial reconstruction surgery first, although they defended themselves by saying that Isabelle's face was too badly damaged for this procedure. Many others questioned the impact of the transplant on a person's sense of identity. If you look like someone else, does this affect your sense of who you are? What about the effect on those who knew the donor? Was Isabelle psychologically the right candidate for this surgery, given that she had effectively attempted suicide?

ISABELLE'S STORY

Isabelle, however, has no doubts about what the surgeons did for her. Weeks after the operation she told journalists that she regarded her new face as a "miracle" and "already beautiful". In 2007 she described the odd sensation of having a stranger's mouth, and how one of her ambitions was to learn how to kiss again. She revealed that it was through the unwanted attentions of the British tabloid press that she discovered her donor had committed suicide, but that, because Isabelle had also tried to kill herself, she felt a strong connection to the dead woman whom she described as her "twin sister".

GET THE FACTS STRAIGHT

Two more partial face transplants - one in China and another one in France - have followed the groundbreaking surgery on Isabelle Dinoire. Some transplant surgeons believe they can go further still and transplant a whole face from a donor to a recipient.This would have obvious applications for someone who had, for example, lost all of their skin and features as a result of severe burns. Surgeons who believe the procedure is possible say it would involve transplanting skin and fatty tissue, and attaching this to the recipient's underlying facial muscles. Those who disagree say that muscle would need to be transplanted too, which would be extremely difficult to graft onto a new face.

► Isabelle Dinoire after her face transplant.

NEW BREAKTHROUGHS

NEW PROCEDURES, treatments and organs for transplant have amazed people around the world since organ transplantation took off in the mid-20th century. There is every reason to think that these achievements will continue in this innovative area of medical science.

▲ Steve Martin in The Man with Two Brains, a 1983 science-fiction comedy about brain transplantation. Some people think, controversially, that such transplants may one day become a medical reality.

OF MICE AND WOMEN

At some point in the future, the uterus may join the list of organs that surgeons can transplant. In 2003, researchers in Sweden succeeded in transplanting uteri (the plural of uterus) from one group of mice to another, and producing healthy offspring.

Human uteri are much more complex than those in mice, so the prospect of carrying out the procedure in women is a long way off. However, women who could benefit include those born without a uterus, or those whose uterus has been damaged by cancer.

INDUCED TOLERANCE

Other researchers are concentrating their efforts on improving the treatment of organ rejection. One area of research is a process called induced tolerance, which builds on findings dating back to the 1950s that showed how newborn babies' immune systems do not recognise and attack foreign material. The theory behind this is that our immune systems learn to reject foreign matter, and so might learn to tolerate it, too. One way of doing this involves giving patients infusions of a donor's bone marrow cells before transplanting the donor's organ, to reduce the chances of rejection.

TAKE HEART

In 2006, two developments gave new hope to heart transplant patients. The first was the way a 12-year-old girl's heart recovered, ten years after her original transplant. The donor organ sat in the chest cavity beside the girl's own heart, which healed over this period.

The second development was a new device to keep a donor heart beating and supplied with blood during its transport to the recipient. The machine gives transplant units more time, and could lead to a considerable increase in the number of hearts which can be transplanted.

FACING THE ISSUES
BRAIN TRANSPLANTS?

The idea of brain transplants stretches back to Mary Shelley's 19th-century gothic novel *Frankenstein*. Some people, such as Professor Robert White of the University of Cleveland, USA, believe such transplants could happen in real life.

Since the 1970s, White has experimented with transplanting the brains of dogs into other dogs, and monkey heads onto different monkey bodies. In 2000, he reported an experiment in which a monkey with a transplanted brain could see, hear, taste and smell. White believes this research could one day benefit people with paralysed bodies. Others in the scientific community fundamentally disagree with White's work.

Dr Stephen Rose of the UK's Open University denied such experiments were transplants at all; instead, he said, it was merely keeping a severed head alive with another animal's blood circulation. "I cannot see any medical grounds for doing this," Rose said.

GLOSSARY

bone marrow: Body tissue in the middle of certain bones.

cell: The basic unit from which all living things are made.

cornea: The transparent layer that covers the front part of the eye.

developing world: A term for generally poor countries that have limited amounts of industry and technology.

dialysis: The process of filtering and cleaning the blood.

donor: Someone who donates blood, tissue, cells or organs, either when alive or after death.

embryo: A very early stage in the development of human or animal life, while still in the uterus of the mother.

ethics: Ideas about what is morally right and wrong.

equality: Treating people the same regardless of their sex, race or condition.

graft: Another word for transplant.

heart: The organ that acts as a pump to circulate the blood.

heart valve: A flap inside the heart that opens and closes to control blood flow.

immune system: The body's natural defence system.

immunosuppressants: Drugs which stop the immune system from rejecting donor organs.

kidney: The organ that removes waste chemicals from the blood. Humans have two kidneys.

liver: The organ that breaks down toxins and old blood cells, stores fats and produces vital chemicals.

lungs: The organ that takes oxygen into the bloodstream and removes carbon dioxide. Like kidneys, we have two lungs.

pancreas: The organ that controls blood sugar levels.

presumed consent: A national system in which everyone is considered a willing donor unless they specifically register a refusal while alive.

recipient: A patient who receives a donated body organ.

rejection: The process in which the immune system attacks a donor organ as foreign matter.

stem cell: A cell with the potential to develop into any type of cell in the body.

tissue: A group of cells that carry out the same function, such as muscle tissue.

transplant tourist: Someone who buys an organ – often illegally – from someone else.

uterus: The organ in the female body which houses and feeds the developing offspring until birth.

virus: A micro-organism that uses the living cells of an animal or plant to reproduce.

WHO (World Health Organization): An agency of the United Nations, established in 1948 to promote health and tackle disease around the world.

xenotransplantation: The use of animal organs, instead of human ones, for transplant.

Websites

American Red Cross
www.redcross.org/donate/tissue/relgstmt.html
This site contains the views of the world's major religions on organ transplantation.

Eurotransplant International Foundation
www.eurotransplant.nl
The Eurotransplant International Foundation co-ordinates organ donation procedures in seven European countries.

The Face Trust
www.thefacetrust.org
Website of a charity set up to fund research into treatment – including transplants – for people with severe facial injuries.

National Kidney Research Fund
www.nkrf.org.uk
This UK charity raises awareness of kidney disease and funds research.

Organ Donor
www.organdonor.gov
Facts and figures on organ donation and transplantation in the USA.

Transplant Australia
www.transplant.org.au
The website for organ donors and transplant patients in Australia.

Every effort has been made by the Publishers to ensure that the websites in this book are suitable for children, that they are of the highest educational value, and that they contain no inappropriate or offensive material. However, because of the nature of the Internet, it is impossible to guarantee that the contents of these sites will not be altered. We strongly advise that Internet access is supervised by a responsible adult.

INDEX

Here are the lists of contents for each title in *Science in the News*:

CLIMATE CHANGE

WHAT IS CLIMATE CHANGE? • CLIMATE CHANGE SCIENCE • CLIMATE SCIENCE HISTORY
CLIMATE CHANGE IN THE PAST • CAUSES OF CLIMATE CHANGE • CARBON DIOXIDE EMISSIONS
THE EFFECTS OF CLIMATE CHANGE • CLIMATE CHANGE REPORTS • PIONEER PRESSURE GROUPS
CLIMATE-CHANGE SUMMITS • GOVERNMENT REACTIONS • NEW INDUSTRIAL NATIONS
CONTINUING PROTESTS • AGAINST THE FLOW • CARBON REDUCTION • PREDICTING THE FUTURE
RESPONDING TO CLIMATE CHANGE

ORGAN TRANSPLANTATION

INTRODUCTION • IN THE BEGINNING • WORLD FIRSTS • ORGAN CRISIS • PRESUMED CONSENT
LIFE FROM LIFE • RELIGION & CULTURE • ARTIFICIAL ORGANS • XENOTRANSPLANTATION
STEM CELL RESEARCH • THE RIGHT TO AN ORGAN? • TRANSPLANT TOURISTS • ORGAN SELLERS
REGULATING THE TRADE • POST-OPERATIVE LIFE • FACE TRANSPLANTS • NEW BREAKTHROUGHS

COSMETIC SURGERY

INTRODUCTION • ANCIENT ORIGINS • THE FIRST AND SECOND WORLD WARS
FROM HOLLYWOOD TO THE HIGH STREET • SURGICAL TREATMENTS • NON-SURGICAL TREATMENTS
THE BENEFITS • THE RISKS • SURGERY ADDICTS • TEENAGE SURGERY • CHECKS AND BALANCES
THE SURGEONS • VIEWING FIGURES • "THE BEAUTY MYTH" • BOOM AND BUST
ALTERNATIVES • FACING THE FUTURE

NUCLEAR POWER

WHAT IS NUCLEAR POWER? • THE HISTORY OF NUCLEAR POWER
WHO USES NUCLEAR POWER? • NUCLEAR FUELS • NUCLEAR POWER STATIONS • NUCLEAR REACTOR TYPES
NUCLEAR POWER FOR TRANSPORT • NUCLEAR WASTE • BUILDING AND DECOMMISSIONING
NUCLEAR SAFETY • THE CHERNOBYL DISASTER • TERROR THREATS • ROGUE STATES
ANTI-NUCLEAR CAMPAIGNS • NUCLEAR POWER PLANS
NUCLEAR FUSION • THE NUCLEAR FUTURE

GENETICS

GENETIC MODIFICATION • DARWIN – FROM MONKEY TO MAN • IN THE GENES
A MASTER-RACE – A BREED APART? • ANIMAL ODDITIES • DNA – A CODE FOR LIVING
THE CHANGING CODE • RECESSIVE GENES – A HIDDEN INHERITANCE • ARE GM CROPS FRANKENSTEIN FOODS?
DANGEROUS MEDDLING? • MAKING MONSTERS? • "GENETIC FINGERPRINTS" • TRACING YOUR ROOTS• NATURE AND NUTURE
ALTERED INHERITANCE • CLONING – A CARBON COPY? • A LEGACY OR TIMEBOMB?

MAKING NEW LIFE

CREATING LIFE • THE MAGIC OF LIFE • MOTHERS AND SONS • ARTIFICIAL INSEMINATION
PARENTAL RESPONSIBILITY • IVF – THE TEST TUBE BABY • MULTIPLE PREGNANCIES • THE GIFT OF LIFE
SURROGACY – TWO MOTHERS? • TOO OLD FOR PARENTHOOD? • CHECKING PROGRESS
SONS OR DAUGHTERS? • SAVIOUR SIBLINGS • FROZEN FOR THE FUTURE • WHAT IS A CLONE?
HUMAN CLONES • CREATING LIFE IN THE FUTURE